HOLIDAY HISTORY
DIWALI

by Nandini Nayar

pogo

Ideas for Parents and Teachers

Pogo Books let children practice reading informational text while introducing them to nonfiction features such as headings, labels, sidebars, maps, and diagrams, as well as a table of contents, glossary, and index.

Carefully leveled text with a strong photo match offers early fluent readers the support they need to succeed.

Before Reading

- "Walk" through the book and point out the various nonfiction features. Ask the student what purpose each feature serves.
- Look at the glossary together. Read and discuss the words.

Read the Book

- Have the child read the book independently.
- Invite him or her to list questions that arise from reading.

After Reading

- Discuss the child's questions. Talk about how he or she might find answers to those questions.
- Prompt the child to think more. Ask: There are interesting stories behind the festival of Diwali. Do you know of stories connected to other festivals or celebrations?

Pogo Books are published by Jump!
5357 Penn Avenue South
Minneapolis, MN 55419
www.jumplibrary.com

Library of Congress Cataloging-in-Publication Data

Names: Nayar, Nandini, author.
Title: Diwali / by Nandini Nayar.
Description: Minneapolis, MN: Jump!, Inc., 2023.
Series: Holiday history | Includes index.
Audience: Ages 7-10
Identifiers: LCCN 2022025943 (print)
LCCN 2022025944 (ebook)
ISBN 9798885241250 (hardcover)
ISBN 9798885241267 (paperback)
ISBN 9798885241274 (ebook)
Subjects: LCSH: Divali—Juvenile literature.
Classification: LCC BL1239.82.D58 N39 2023 (print)
LCC BL1239.82.D58 (ebook)
DDC 294.5/36—dc23/eng/20220725
LC record available at https://lccn.loc.gov/2022025943
LC ebook record available at https://lccn.loc.gov/2022025944

Editor: Eliza Leahy
Designer: Molly Ballanger

Photo Credits: Shutterstock, cover, 6-7; brewing thought/Shutterstock, 1; MRS.Siwaporn/Shutterstock, 3; reddees/Shutterstock, 4; Raksha Shelare/Shutterstock, 5; Indiapicture/Alamy, 8-9; SMDSS/Shutterstock, 10; Kedar Diwakar Mandakhalikar/iStock, 11; Santhosh Varghese/Shutterstock, 12-13; StockImageFactory.com/Shutterstock, 13, 23; uniquely india/Getty, 14-15; Universal Images Group North America LLC/Alamy, 16-17; REUTERS/Henry Nicholls/Alamy, 18; Sean Drakes/Getty, 19; Michael Lee/Getty, 20-21.

Printed in the United States of America at Corporate Graphics in North Mankato, Minnesota.

TABLE OF CONTENTS

CHAPTER 1

MANY STORIES

In one **Hindu** story, Rama was the prince of Ayodhya, India. Ravana was the king of Sri Lanka. He kidnapped Rama's wife, Sita. Rama formed an army. They won against Ravana. They brought Sita back.

Rama

People welcomed them back. They lit diyas. Diyas are oil lamps. They became **symbols** of the **victory** of light over darkness.

diya

Rama and Sita's story is one of many celebrated during the festival of Diwali. Diwali also celebrates Lord Krishna's defeat of the **demon** Narakasura. It celebrates the Hindu goddess Lakshmi and god Ganesha, too.

DID YOU KNOW?

Rama and Krishna are **incarnations** of the Hindu god Vishnu. Hindus believe that Vishnu fights evil.

Ganesha

Lakshmi

CHAPTER 1

Several other stories are celebrated during Diwali. All have a similar **theme**. They celebrate the victory of light over darkness and good over evil.

Diwali follows the Hindu calendar. It falls between late October and early November each year. It is known as the Festival of Lights. Diyas are a common **tradition**!

WHAT DO YOU THINK?

Yellow and gold are popular Diwali colors. Why do you think these colors are common during Diwali?

CHAPTER 2

DIWALI TRADITIONS

Diwali is a time for families to gather. They prepare for weeks. They clean. They decorate. They design rangolis. They use colorful powder or flower petals.

rangoli

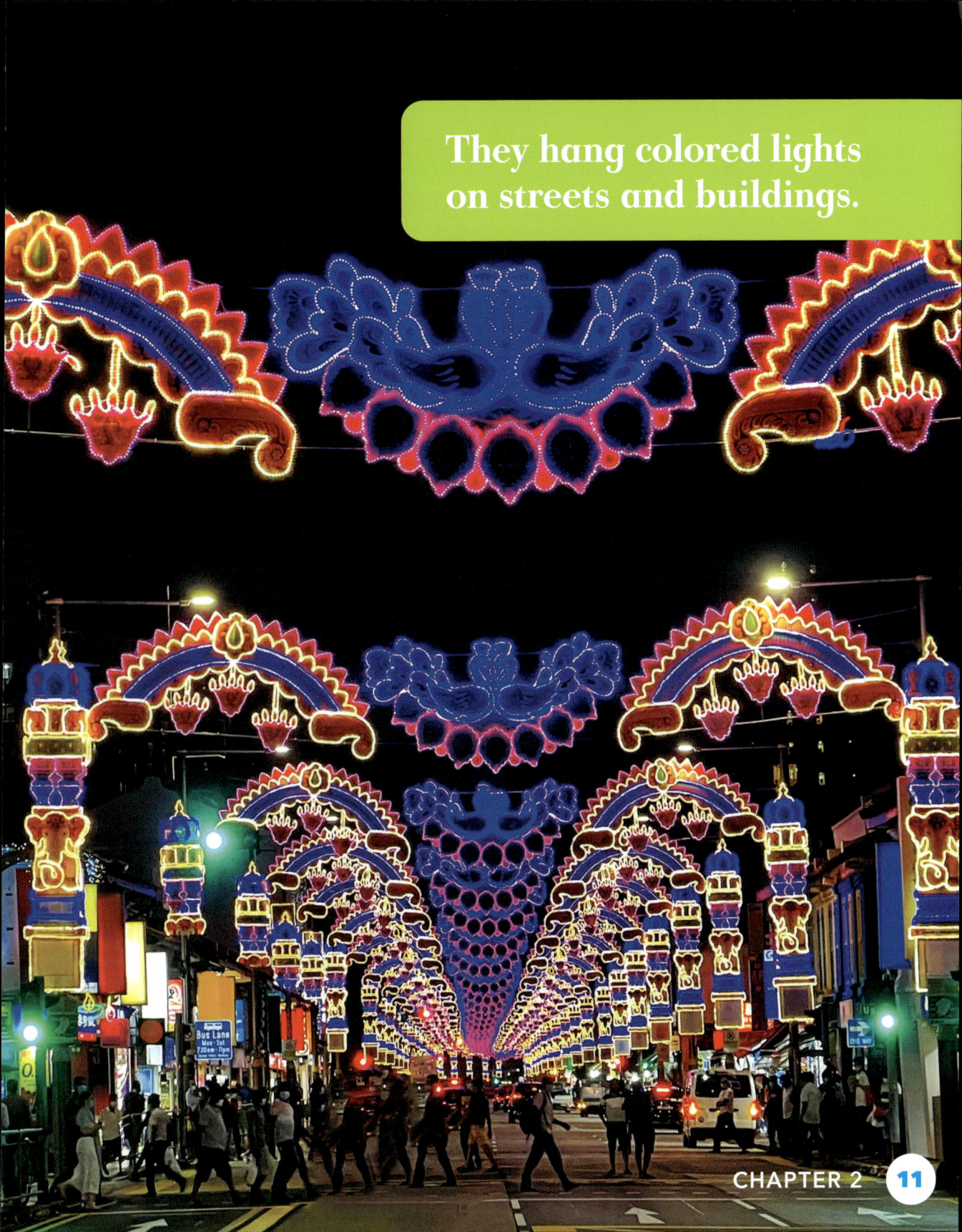

They hang colored lights on streets and buildings.

syrup ·····▶

People make sweets. They use milk, sugar, **ghee**, and flour. Gulab jamun is one kind. These fried dough balls are soaked in syrup.

People offer sweets to the gods before eating them. Boxes of sweets are popular gifts during Diwali.

sweets

People wear new clothes. They visit **temples**. They **worship** gods. They sing **hymns**. They hang **garlands** of flowers over doors. These are meant to welcome Lakshmi. People believe Lakshmi visits homes during Diwali.

TAKE A LOOK!

Diwali takes place over five days. What happens on each day? Take a look!

DAY 1 People buy items like utensils and jewelry. It is considered good luck!

DAY 2 People celebrate Krishna's defeat of Narakasura. They enjoy **ritual** baths.

DAY 3 People worship Ganesha and Lakshmi.

DAY 4 In many parts of India, this is the beginning of the Hindu New Year. People visit with family and friends. They give one another gifts.

DAY 5 The last day of Diwali celebrates the **bond** between brothers and sisters. Sisters pray for the long lives of their brothers. Brothers promise to protect their sisters.

People have different Diwali traditions. Why? It depends on who is celebrating and where. But most celebrations include diyas. In the evenings, people light sparklers. They also set off fireworks.

WHAT DO YOU THINK?

Diwali is mainly celebrated by Hindus. But people of other Indian religions, like Sikhism and Jainism, celebrate it, too. Some of their traditions are different. Why do you think this is?

sparkler

CHAPTER 3

DIWALI AROUND THE WORLD

People around the world celebrate Diwali. The celebration in London is popular. There are food stalls. People watch music and dance performances.

London

Trinidad and Tobago

In Trinidad and Tobago, people celebrate Divali Nagar. This event has food. People visit clothing stalls. There are performances. Fireworks light up the sky.

In the United States, fairs are part of Diwali celebrations. Food stalls are, too. Temples and homes are lit up. Some cities have fireworks.

Do you celebrate Diwali? If not, would you like to? Why?

New York City

CHAPTER 3 21

QUICK FACTS & TOOLS

DIWALI PLACE OF ORIGIN

QUICK FACTS

Dates: late October to early November

Place of Origin: Ayodhya, India

Common Symbols: diyas, rangoli, Ganesha, Lakshmi, sweets, fireworks, jewelry

Foods: laddoo, barfi, jalebi, gulab jamun

Traditions: decorating homes and shops with lights and rangoli, worshipping gods, lighting lamps outside homes, lighting fireworks, taking ritual baths

GLOSSARY

bond: A close connection with or strong feeling for someone.

demon: A devil or an evil spirit.

garlands: Wreaths of flowers and leaves.

ghee: A special form of butter that has been cooked and is made especially in India.

Hindu: Of or relating to Hinduism, a religion and philosophy practiced mainly in India. Hindus worship many gods and believe in reincarnation.

hymns: Songs that praise a god or gods.

incarnations: Physical forms of gods on Earth.

national holiday: A legal holiday established by the central government of a nation.

ritual: An act or series of acts that is always performed in the same way, usually as part of a religious or social ceremony.

symbols: Objects or designs that stand for, suggest, or represent something else.

temples: Buildings used for worshipping a god or gods.

theme: The main subject or idea of a piece of writing or a talk.

tradition: A custom, idea, or belief that is handed down from one generation to the next.

victory: A win in a battle, war, game, or contest.

worship: To show respect to a god or gods.

INDEX

TO LEARN MORE

Finding more information is as easy as 1, 2, 3.

1 **Go to www.factsurfer.com**

2 **Enter "Diwali" into the search box.**

3 **Choose your book to see a list of websites.**

FACT SURFER